We Work in
Space

Angela Aylmore

www.heinemann.co.uk/library
Visit our website to find out more information about **Heinemann Library** books.

To order:
☎ Phone 44 (0) 1865 888066
▤ Send a fax to 44 (0) 1865 314091
▭ Visit the Heinemann Bookshop at www.heinemann.co.uk/library to browse our catalogue and order online.

First published in Great Britain by Heinemann Library, Halley Court, Jordan Hill, Oxford OX2 8EJ, part of Harcourt Education.
Heinemann is a registered trademark of Harcourt Education Ltd.

Editorial: Isabel Thomas and Sarah Chappelow
Design: Jo Hinton-Malivoire and bigtop
Picture Research: Erica Newbery
Production: Duncan Gilbert

Originated by RMW
Printed and bound in China by South China Printing Company

ISBN: 978 0 431 16490 8 (hardback)
10 09 08 07
10 9 8 7 6 5 4 3 2 1

ISBN: 978 0 431 16495 3 (paperback)
11 10 09 08 07
10 9 8 7 6 5 4 3 2 1

British Library Cataloguing in Publication Data
Aylmore, Angela
We work in space. - (Where we work)
629.4'5
A full catalogue record for this book is available from the British Library.

Acknowledgements
The publishers would like to thank the following for permission to reproduce photographs:
Alamy pp. **7** (Phototake Inc.), **14** (Hugh Threlfall), **18–19** (Bill Howe); Corbis pp. **6** (Roger Ressmeyer), **10** (Jim Sugar); Getty Images pp. **4** (Photodisc), **13** (Photodisc), **21** (Photodisc); Science Photo Library/NASA pp. **8**, **9**, **12**, **15**, **16**, **17**, **20**.

Quiz pp. **22–23**: **astronaut** (Getty/Photodisc), **brush and comb** (Corbis/DK Limited), **doctor** (Getty Images/Photodisc), **firefighter helmet** (Corbis), **ladder** (Corbis/Royalty Free), **scrubs** (Corbis), **space food** (Alamy/Hugh Threlfall), **stethoscope** (Getty Images/Photodisc), **thermometer** (Getty Images/Photodisc).

Cover photograph of an astronaut reproduced with permission of Alamy/Bill Howe.

Every effort has been made to contact copyright holders of any material reproduced in this book. Any omissions will be rectified in subsequent printings if notice is given to the publishers.

The paper used to print this book comes from sustainable resources.

Some words are shown in bold, **like this**. They are explained in the glossary on page 24.

Contents

Welcome to space!

This is a **space station**.
It is a very long way from Earth.

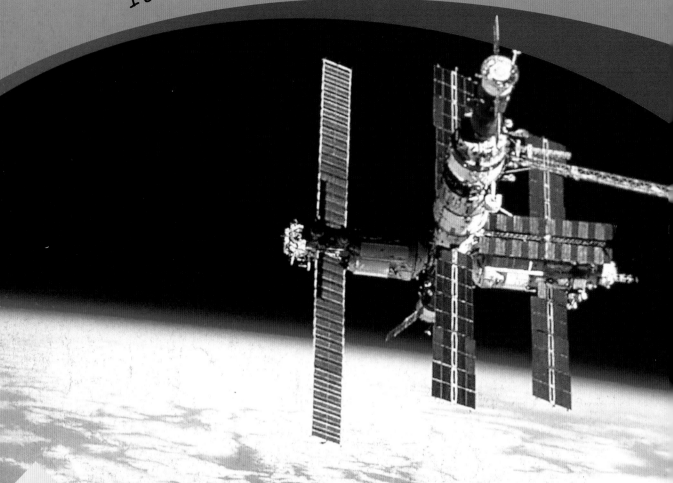

Who do you think works here?

5

Working in space

We are astronauts.
We work in the **space station**.

We find out
about the **stars**
and **planets**
in space.

Lift off!

We travel into space in a **shuttle**.

5 4 3 2 1
Lift off!

8

The shuttle takes us to the **space station**.

Floating around

Being in space is very different to being on Earth.

Getting dressed

In the **space station** we wear ordinary clothes.

Time to eat

We eat dried food
from special packets.

15

We do **experiments** to find out more about space.

16

Today we want to see
how well these plants
are growing in space.

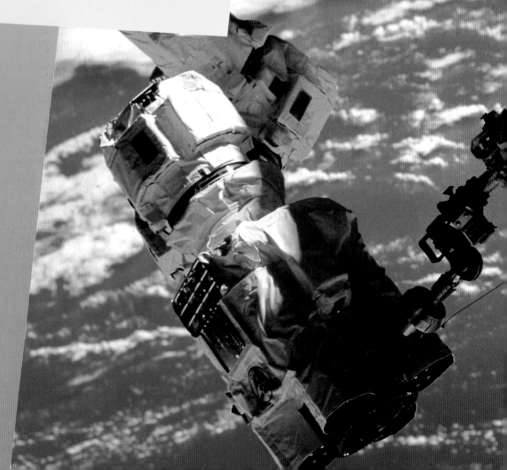

Sometimes we have to go outside to fix the **space station**.

18

This part of the job is dangerous.
We have to be very careful!

Back home

When we have finished our work, we go back to Earth.

The parachute helps our **shuttle** to slow down.

parachute

There is a lot to learn about space. We hope to go back soon!

Quiz

space food

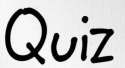

Do you want to be an astronaut? Which of these things would you need?

stethoscope

spacesuit

helmet

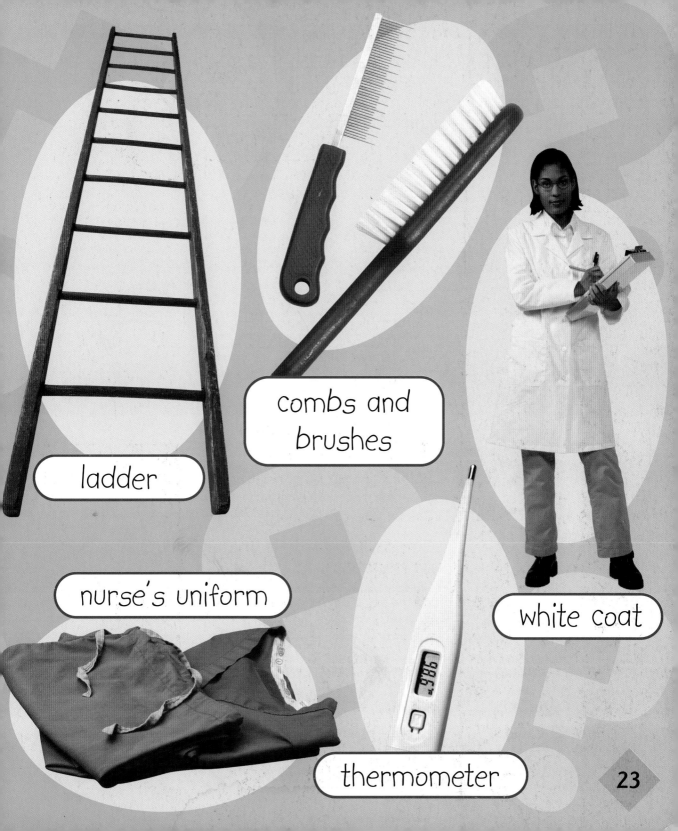

ladder

combs and
brushes

nurse's uniform

thermometer

white coat

Glossary

experiment test to find things out

planet the Earth is a plant. There are lots of other planets in the sky.

shuttle rocket that takes astronauts into space

space station place where astronauts live in space

stars bright lights you can see in the sky at night

Index

Notes for adults

This series supports the young child's exploration of their learning environment and their knowledge and understanding of their world. The following Early Learning Goals are relevant to the series:

• Respond to significant experiences, showing a range of feelings where appropriate.
• Find out about events they observe.
• Ask questions about why things happen and how things work.
• Find out and identify the uses of everyday technology to support their learning.

The series shows the different jobs professionals do in four different environments. There are opportunities to compare and contrast the jobs and provide an understanding of what each entails.

The books will help the child to extend their vocabulary, as they will hear new words. Some of the words that may be new to them in **We Work in Space** are *astronaut, space shuttle, experiment, planets, stars,* and *space station*. Since the words are used in context in the book this should enable the young child to gradually incorporate them into their own vocabulary.

Follow-up activities
The child could role play situations in a space shuttle. They could imagine what it would be like during take off and landing, and what astronauts might do while they are in space. The child could also record what they have found out by drawing, painting, or tape recording their experiences.